Cinzia Valigi

The Vatican

St. Peter's Basilica
The Sistine Chapel
Vatican Museums

CENTRO STAMPA EDITORIALE

plurigraf

PERSEUS

PG-VAT1-01

Index

© Copyright
CASA EDITRICE PERSEUS - PLURIGRAF collection
Published and printed by Centro Stampa Editoriale, Sesto Fiorentino, (Fi).

Introduction

Vatican City is the smallest independent state in the world. It was founded in 1929 as the seat of the Pope and hence of the Government of the Roman Catholic Church. The Vatican, which covers an area of 440,000 square metres, is the seat of the Successor of Peter, and as such the moral and spiritual centre of Christianity. Yet it has not always been the seat of the Papacy: initially the Popes occupied the Lateran Palace donated to them by the Emperor Constantine, who also built the Lateran Basilica. During the Middle Ages, however, the buildings of the Lateran were almost completely destroyed; the Popes therefore moved to the area adjacent to St. Peter's Basilica, built, again by Constantine, over the tomb of the first of the Apostles.

We approach the Vatican by making our way along the broad Via della Conciliazione flanked by obelisks, which leads into St. Peter's Square, a masterpiece of Bernini. Here we are welcomed by the symbolic ''embrace'' of Bernini's colonnade surrounding the piazza. At the centre of the elliptical colonnade, consisting of 284 columns surmounted by statues of saints, rises the Egyptian obelisk of red granite from the Circus of Caligula and Nero. It is flanked by twin fountains formed by enormous monolithic basins of oriental granite: the one to the right erected by Maderno in 1613, and the one to the left by Bernini in 1675.

But the chief protagonist of the piazza is the wonderful Basilica of St. Peter itself. This is the modern successor to the original Early Christian basilica built by Constantine over the tomb of the Saint. This was a large and imposing building, but it became progressively delapidated in the course of the Middle Ages and it was therefore decided to replace it with a new basilica which was begun in 1506. The initial designs for the new St. Peter's were produced by Bramante, and he was followed as architect successively by Raphael, Baldassare Peruzzi, Antonio da Sangallo and Michelangelo. The latter, recurring to Bramante's original plan, conceived of a huge and monumental Greek-cross basilica surmounted by a double-shell dome. Originally hemispherical, the dome was subsequently elongated by Fontana and Della Porta. In the early years of the 17th century, Maderno, on the commission of Pope Paul V, transformed the original Greek-cross plan (with arms of equal length) into a Latin-cross plan by a prolongation of the nave which involved the destruction of precious artistic treasures. Maderno also designed and erected the façade in the space of five months. In the mid-17th century Gian Lorenzo Bernini not only designed the piazza onto which it looks, enclosed by two great hemicycles of columns, but embellished the interior of the basilica in the baroque taste, conferring on it the sumptuous, appearance that characterises it today.

St. Peter's Square and Basilica.

St. Peter's Basilica

Preceded by Bernini's imposing flight of stairs, the façade of the Basilica is flanked by the statues of Saints Peter and Paul. It is decorated with a series of elegant balconies, of which the central one is the so-called **Loggia delle Benedizioni**: it is from this balcony that the Pope imparts his "urbi et orbi" blessing to the numerous faithful thronging St. Peter's Square. Below, five entrances lead into the magnificent **Vestibule** by Maderno (1608-13). It is decorated with wonderful stuccoes and mosaics, including the **Mosaic of the Navicella** placed in the lunette over the central door; designed by Giotto, it represents the ship with the disciples navigating an agitated sea and symbolises the stability of the Church even in the face of adversity. The artist's signature is no longer visible due to the various restorations to which the mosaic has been subject over the years. To the extreme left of the Vestibule is the **equestrian statue of Charlemagne** (who was crowned here in 800), while to the far right, behind glass doors, is that of the **Emperor Constantine**, sculpted by Bernini.

Five doors lead into the Basilica from the Vestibule. The oldest of these is the central one; the bronze doors date to the 15th century and are the work of Filarete. They are decorated with bas-reliefs of the martyrdoms of Saints Peter and Paul, and are a masterpiece of Renaissance bronzesmith's work. To its left is the **Door of Death** by Giacomo Manzù, on which John XXIII is portrayed, while to its right is the **Door of the Sacraments** sculpted by Venanzio Crocetti. Next to it is the **Door** representing **Good** and **Evil** installed here in 1977. The last door to the right is the walled-up door of the **Porta Santa**, famous throughout the world, which the Pope opens symbolically using a ceremonial hammer to mark the beginning of Jubilee Years.

St. Peter's Square from the St. Peter's Dome.

Collonnade in St. Peter's Square (Bernini).

St. Peter's Basilica - Detail.

St. Peter's Square- Detail. ➤

St. Peter's Square.   *Via della Conciliazione.*

1) Obelisk
2) Fountain
3) Fountain
4) Steps
5) Statue of St. Peter
6) Statue of St. Paul
7) Portico, or Atrium of the Basilica
8) Main Entrance Door
9) Statue of Charlemagne
10) Equestrian Statue of Constantine
11) The Bronze Door
12) The Holy Door
13) Holy Water Stoup
14) Holy Water Stoup
15) Porphyry Disc
16) Chapel of the Pietà
17) Chapel of the Relics
18) Tomb of Leo XII
19) Tomb of Christina of Sweden
20) Chapel of St. Sebastian
20) Monument of Pope Pius XI
21) Tomb of Countess Mathilda of Canossa
22) Tomb of Pope Innocent XII
23) Chapel of the Blessed Sacrament
23) Tabernacle
24) Altar of St. Francis
25) Organ
26) Tomb of Gregory XIII
27) Tomb of Gregory XIV
28) Gregorian Chapel
28) Madonna del Soccorso
29) Tomb of Gregory XVI
30) « The Communion of St. Jerome »
31) Altar of St. Basil
32) Tomb of Benedict XIV
33) Altar of St. Wenceslaus
34) Altar of S. Processus and S. Martinianus
35) Altar of St. Erasmus
36) Altar of the Boat
37) Tomb of Clement XIII
38) Chapel of St. Michael
39) Altar of S. Petronilla
40) Tomb of Clement X
41) « St. Peter raising Tabitha from the Dead »
42) St. Peter's Chair
43) Tomb of Urban VIII
44) Tomb of Paul III
45) Michelangelo's Dome
46) Canopy
47) Papal Altar
48) The Confession
48) Statue of Pius VI
49) Statue of St. Longinus
50) Statue of St. Peter
51) Statue of t. Helena
52) Statue of St. Veronica
53) Statue of St. Andrew
54) Tomb of Pope Alexander VIII
55) St. Peter's Altar
56) Chapel of the Column
57) Altar of St. Leo the Great
58) Tomb of Pope Alexander VII
59) Altar of the Sacred Heart
60) Altar of St. Thomas
61) Altar of the Crucifixion of St. Peter
62) Altar of S. Marziale and S. Valeria
63) Tomb of Pope P us VIII
64) Sacristy
65) Altar of the Lie
66) The Clementine Chapel
67) Tomb of Pius VII
68) Altar of the Transfiguration
69) Tomb of Pope Leon XI
70) Tomb of Pope Innocent XI
71) Chapel of the Choir
72) Monument of Pius X
73) Tomb of Innocent VIII
74) Chapel of the Presentation
75) Monument of Benedict XV
76) Monument of Maria Clementina Sobiesky
77) The Stuart Monument
78) Baptistery

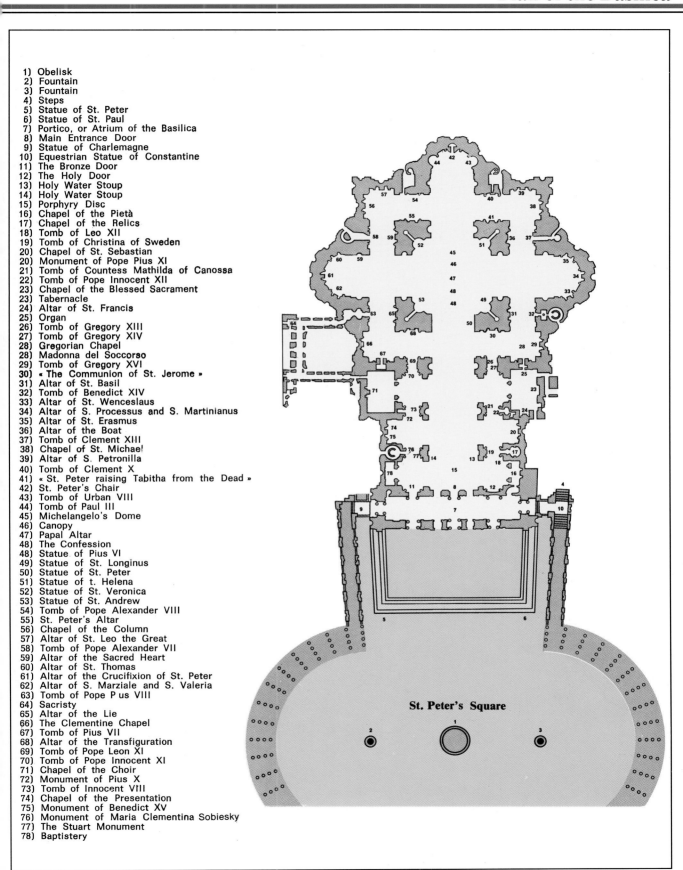

St. Peter's Square

Interior of the Basilica

On entering the Basilica, we are immediately overawed by its size and grandeur: the largest sacred edifice in the world, it was conceived to celebrate the sacrality of the Catholic Church, and as such is full of holy relics and wonderful works of art in a splendid fusion of the Renaissance and Baroque. The enormous size of the statues can be gauged from the putti supporting the two **holy water stoups,** placed at the beginning of the nave and sculpted by Francesco Moderati and Giuseppe Lironi in the early 18th century.

Worth noting is the large **disc of red porphyry** set into the floor; it comes from the old basilica.

Against the last pillar to the right of the central nave is the venerated **bronze statue of St. Peter,** sculpted by Arnolfo di Cambio in the 13th century. It is the custom for pilgrims to kiss the feet of the saint as an act of devotion.

St. Peter's Basilica - Interior.

Holy water stoup (F. Moderati, G. Lironi).

RIGHT AISLE

CHAPEL OF THE PIETÀ - The first chapel in the right aisle takes its name from the famous statue of the **Pietà** by Michelangelo, sculpted by the artist at the precocious age of 25 on the occasion of the Jubilee of 1500. Commissioned by a French cardinal, the work, the only one to be signed by the artist, portrays the dead body of Christ lying in the lap of his Mother. Grief, but above all submission to divine will, marks the face of the youthful Virgin who supports the body of her dead Son. Damaged by a lunatic in 1972, the statue has been perfectly restored by the Vatican Laboratory for the Restoration of Works of Art.

Adjacent to the Chapel is the **Spiral Column**, an object of veneration.

CHAPEL OF THE RELICS OR OF THE CRUCIFIX - Designed by Bernini, the chapel is elliptical in form and houses a fine **wooden Crucifix** by Cavallini (13th century). To the left is the **funerary monument of Christina, Queen of Sweden,** by Carlo Fontana; the bas-relief portrays the Queen's abjuration of Protestantism in 1655.

CHAPEL OF ST. SEBASTIAN - It is dedicated to the **Martyrdom of St. Sebastian**, the scene depicted in the mosaic copy of the painting by Domenichino over the altar. To the left is the **bronze statue of Pius XII** by Francesco Messina, while in front is the **monument to Pius XI** by Canonica. In the passage is the **Tomb of Innocent XII;** designed by Ferdinando Fuga, the statue of the Pope is placed between figures of **Charity** and **Justice** by Filippo Valle. To the left is the **Mausoleum of the Contessa Matilde of Canossa**, whose remains were brought here in 1635; the tomb and the statue of Matilde were designed by Bernini. The bas-relief in front of the sarcophagus is by Stefano Speranza, and represents the scene of the emperor Henry IV being absolved from excommunication by Gregory VII in the Castle of Canossa.

CHAPEL OF THE HOLY SACRAMENT - Decorated with gilded stuccoes and closed by an elegant wrought-iron gate (designed by Borromini), it houses Bernini's wonderful gilt bronze **ciborium**, flanked by two bronze angels; it was inspired by Bramante's famous Tempietto at San Pietro in Montorio. Behind is a wonderful altarpiece of the **Trinity** by Pietro da Cortona. Also worth noting in the chapel is the ancient wooden organ and, on the altar to the right, a mosaic copy of Domenichino's painting: **The Ecstasy of St. Francis.**

In the passage beyond, to the right, is the **monument to Pope Gregory XIII** by Camillo Rusconi, flanked by statues of Religion and Wisdom. To the left is the tomb of **Gregory XIV,** while at the foot of the aisle is the altar with a mosaic copy of Domenichino's painting: **The Communion of St. Jerome.**

"La Pietà" (Michelangelo).

Left-hand page: The Chapel of the "Pietà".

"La Pietà" - *Details.*

GREGORIAN CHAPEL - Built by Giacomo Della Porta in 1583, it is named after Pope Gregory XIII who founded it. Over the altar is an 11th century icon of the Virgin: the **Madonna del Soccorso**. The chapel is decorated with precious mosaics and splendid marbles which confer on it a very sumptuous appearance. The Gregorian Chapel owes its design to two of the most distinguished architects of the period, Vignola and Giacomo Della Porta (who completed it); but it is uncertain who were the artists of the paintings that decorate it. To the right is the **monument of Pope Gregory XVI** by Luigi Amici (1854).

Before visiting the Transept, we may note in the passage leading to it the **Tomb of Benedict XIV,** sculpted by Pietro Bacci in the mid-18th century. On the altar to the left is a fine mosaic copy of the painting of the **Mass of St. Basil** by Subleyras, commissioned by Benedict XIV.

RIGHT TRANSEPT

Mosaic reproductions of paintings by distinguished 17th century artists are placed over the three altars: **St. Wenceslaus, King of Bohemia,** by Caroselli; the **Martyrdom of Saints Processus and Martinianus** by Valentin, the original of which is displayed in the Vatican Picture Gallery; and the **Martyrdom of St. Erasmus** by Poussin. In the passage to the Chapel of St. Michael is the **Monument to Clement XIII.** Among the most important and famous of Canova's works, the monument is arranged round the door to the funerary chamber; below, two crouching lions stand guard; the sarcophagus is flanked by statues of Religion and Genius, while above is the statue of the Pope kneeling in prayer.

CHAPEL OF ST. MICHAEL THE ARCHANGEL - The two altars are embellished with mosaic copies of paintings of **St. Michael** by Guido Reni (the original is in the church of Santa Maria della Concezione) and **St. Petronilla** by Guercino.

In the passage to the tribune is the **Monument to Clement X,** designed by Mattia de' Rossi. On the altar to the left is a fine mosaic copy of a painting by Placido Costanzo: **St. Peter raising Tabitha** (1760).

APSE

The apse of the Basilica is dominated by the **Cathedra Petri,** the famous monument of the Throne of St. Peter. This sumptuous baroque complex was sculpted in black bronze and gold by Gian Lorenzo Bernini under the pontificate of Alexander VII. Enclosed within it is the ancient wooden chair encrusted with ivory used, according to tradition, by the Saint. At the foot of the great bronze throne are the four colossal figures of the Doctors of the Church: Saints Ambrose, Augustine, Athanasius and John Chrysostom. The two gilt-bronze angels flanking the throne help to confer grace and brilliance on this vast work conceived by Bernini with the greatest imaginative power. The monument is topped by the magnificient **Glory of angels** in gilded stucco, at the centre of which the Holy Spirit appears in the form of the pentecostal dove.

Two imposing papal tombs are placed to the sides of the apse: the **Monument to Urban VIII,** a masterpiece of 17th century funerary sculpture by Bernini, the black marble sarcophagus flanked by gleaming white marble statues of Justice and Charity; and the **Monument to Paul III** by Guglielmo Della Porta, with the bronze statue of the Farnese Pope, flanked below by marble statues of Justice and Prudence.

In the passage to the Left Transept we find the **Tomb of Alexander** VIII, with allegorical statues of Religion and Prudence. The altar facing it is decorated with a mosaic copy of a painting by Francesco Mancini depicting **St. Peter healing the Lame Man.**

CHAPEL OF THE COLUMN - To the left of the tribune, the Chapel, decorated by Della Porta, takes its name from the **Madonna della Colonna,** a much-venerated icon of the Virgin of great antiquity (it was removed from the old basilica). The Chapel is dominated by Algardi's wonderful high-relief marble altarpiece of the **Meeting between St. Leo and Attila.**

Before beginning our visit to the Left Transept, we may note, in the passage, the imposing **Tomb of Alexander VII,** a sumptuous ensemble of coloured marbles and bronze designed by Bernini towards the end of his life and sculpted with the help of his pupils.

Statue of St. Peter

St. Peter's Chair (Bernini).
Left-hand page: Interior of St. Peter's Dome.

LEFT TRANSEPT

The three altars are embellished with mosaic copies of paintings: to the left, the **Crucifixion of St. Peter**, from the original by Guido Reni now in the Vatican Picture Gallery; at the centre, **St. Joseph protector of the Universal Church,** by Achille Funi; and to the right, the **Incredulity of St. Thomas**, by Vincenzo Camuccini.

The altar facing the entrance to the Sacristy has an altarpiece of the **Punishment of Sapphira**, a mosaic copy of the original by Pomarancio. Before entering the Sacristy, we may note the 19th century **Monument to Pius VIII** sculpted by Pietro Tenerani. Below it is the entrance to the Sacristy, built by Carlo Marchionni as an annex to the basilica on behalf of Pope Pius VI in the later 18th century. Making our way along the long corridor which leads into the Sacristy and where a tablet records the 147 popes buried in the Basilica, we come to the **statue of St. Andrew** in the vestibule. Adjacent to it is the entrance to the octagonal **Common Sacristy,**

St. Peter's Dome.
Left-hand page: Interior of St. Peter's Dome.

with columns from Hadrian's Villa. It leads in turn, to the left, into the **Sacristy of the Canons.** Since 1974 a part of the Sacristy has been occupied by the **Museum of the Treasury of St. Peter** which contains precious liturgical objects and interesting remains from the old basilica; a large part of the material on display consists of donations made by the faithful over the centuries. Particularly worth noting are: the wonderful **Crux Vaticana** (6th century), a gold cross richly studded with gems donated by the Byzantine Emperor Justin II; the 4th century **Roman sarcophagus of Junius Bassus,** praefectus urbis; the marble **Ciborium** sculpted by Donatello; the **bronze funerary monument of Sixtus IV,** a masterpiece of the art of Pallaiolo dating to 1493; a gilt **Cockerel** placed on top of the Basilica's bell-tower from the 8th to the end of the 16th century; and the **Tiara,** studded with precious stones, with which the statue of St. Peter was crowned on feast-days.

CLEMENTINE CHAPEL - Built by Giacomo Della Porta, it has over its altar a mosaic copy of a painting by Andrea Sacchi depicting an episode from the life of Gregory the Great; the remains of the Saint are placed below the altar.

The Chapel also houses the **Tomb of Pius VII** (the Pope kept prisoner by Napoleon), a frigid work in the neoclassical style by Thorvaldsen.

Left-hand page: The Font (Fontana).

The Altar called "della Bugia".

LEFT AISLE

On entering the left aisle, we may note to the left the altar with a beautiful mosaic copy of Raphael's great **Transfiguration.** Against the third pillar of the aisle we come to the white marble **Monument to Leo XI** sculpted by Algardi; the seated statue of the Pope is placed over a sarcophagus, below which are allegorical figures of Majesty, Liberality and the Kingdom.

It is followed by the **Monument to Innocent XI**, designed by Carlo Maratta; the allegorical statues of Religion and Justice below are by Pierre Monnot.

CHAPEL OF THE CHOIR - It is decorated with magnificient gilding and stucco by Giovanni Battista Ricci. Worth noting is the **Choir** by Giovanni Battista Soria. Over the altar is a fine mosaic of the **Immaculate Conception,** a copy of a painting by Pietro Bianchi.

In the next bay of the aisle, to the left, is the bronze **Tomb of Innocent VIII** by Pollaiuolo, salvaged from the old basilica.

CHAPEL OF THE PRESENTATION - Over the altar is the **Presentation of Mary to the Temple,** a mosaic copy of the original painting by Pomarelli. Below the altar are the remains of St. Pius X. To the left is the **Monument to Benedict XV,** kneeling in prayer.

In the passage between the Chapel of the Presentation and the Baptistery is the Monument to **Maria Clementina Sobieski,** wife of the Old Pretender, James Francis Edward Stuart. Facing it is the **funerary stele of the last of the Stuarts** by Canova.

BAPTISTERY - The last chapel of the left aisle is the Baptistery. The fine **Baptismal Font** (designed by Carlo Fontana) is formed by a large basin, originally the cover of an ancient porphyry sarcophagus which contained the remains of the Emperor Otto II. Over the altar are mosaic copies of paintings by leading exponents of 17th century Mannerism.

THE DOME

After completing our tour of the interior of St. Peter's, we can study in more detail the wonderful dome. The first stage of our ascent is the gallery running round the inside of the dome, from which — at an altitude of 53 metres — we can admire the majestic interior of St. Peter's. Continuing our ascent, we climb a further 300 steps and so reach the top of the dome, at a height of over 100 metres. From here superb panoramic views can be enjoyed not only of St. Peter's Square and its surrounding buildings, but of the whole city of Rome stretching away as far as the Alban Hills and beyond. Behind St. Peter's extend the wonderful **Vatican Gardens.**

The Vatican Crypts

THE VATICAN CRYPTS

The Vatican Crypts (**Grotte Vaticane**) lie below the Basilica, in the area between the Baldacchino and the half-way point of the central nave. They bear tangible witness to almost two millennia in the history of Christianity and the Papacy. A number of Early Christian sarcophagi, numerous remains from the old basilica and the tombs of many Popes are in fact contained in the Crypts, which are divided into two parts. The **Grotte Nuove**, arranged in a semicircle opening out into various chapels, contain the famous and venerated **Tomb of St. Peter,** covered by the **Confession** or **Shrine of Saints Peter and Paul**. Another part of the interspace between the Constantinian basilica and the floor of the present St. Peter's is occupied by the **Grotte Vecchie** (1606). Worth noting are the **Tomb of John XXIII,** visited and revered by pilgrims from all over the world, and the **Tomb of Boniface VIII,** the Pope of the First Jubilee.

Left-hand page: The Altar of the Transfiguration.

Vatican Crypts - Tomb of St. Peter.

The Basilica Treasury. Papal tiara by Arnolfo di Cambio.

Right-hand page:
The Porta Santa from the interior.

The Vatican Palaces

The complex of buildings we are now going to describe represents the most important architectural nucleus extant anywhere both from an artistic and historical viewpoint. During the earlier Middle Ages the Popes resided in the Papal Palace at the Lateran, while the Vatican was used as a spiritual centre and for ceremonial occasions. A modest dwelling had been installed here by Pope Symmachus in the 6th century. It was only used on the occasion of ceremonies — as during the coronation of Charlemagne — and as a refuge of the Popes during the frequent political upheavals of the period. In the 9th century, Leo IV surrounded the tract of territory comprised between St. Peter's and Santo Spirito with a tall circuit of fortified walls, thus transforming the Vatican region into a fortified enclave which took the name of the Leonine City. The Vatican Palace itself was later restored and enlarged by Eugenius III and Celestine III and, on the return of Gregory XI from Avignon, became the official seat of the successor of Peter. The first Conclave was held in it in 1378. Successive Popes in the 15th century resided in it, and the most prestigious artists of the Italian Renaissance were summoned to enlarge and embellish it. Soon the building assumed a quintessentially humanist character and appearance, especially inside. Fra Angelico decorated the walls of the Cappella Niccolina. The humanistically-minded Nicholas V laid the foundations of the Vatican Library, and, later, Sixtus IV built the Sistine Chapel, enlisting the services of Botticelli and other leading Italian painters of the day to decorate its walls. Alexander VI added the Borgia Apartment and commissioned Pinturicchio to fresco its walls towards the end of the century. In 1484 Antonio del Pollaiuolo designed the Palazzetto del Belvedere as a separate garden-house; it was built by Pietrasanta and later, under the pontificate of Julius II, connected by Bramante to the Papal Palace by an elaborate courtyard.

The Pope's Apostolic Palace.

*Right-hand page:
Main Staircase
(Bernini).*

It was Julius II, too, who commissioned the young and precocious Raphael to fresco the suite of rooms known as the **Stanze,** whose construction and initial decoration dated back to the pontificate of Nicholas V. Other great pictorial programmes followed: the frescoing of the ceiling of the Sistine Chapel by Michelangelo (under Julius II) and that of the Logge of Raphael (under Leo X). Under the successive pontificates of Paul III, Pius IV, Pius V, Gregory XIII and Sixtus V, the construction and decoration of the Vatican Palace complex were brought to completion.

The main (official) entrance to the Vatican Palaces is through the **Bronze Portal** to the right of St. Peter's, which admits to the **Scala Regia,** the great ceremonial staircase designed by Bernini for Pope Alexander VII in 1664-66. This takes its name from the **Sala Regia** or throne-room to which it led, and is considered a masterpiece of Bernini's art. Bernini was able by optical means to exploit the narrow and irregular site of the staircase: by the ingenious use of lighting and perspective techniques, and the gradual diminution in the width of the stair, he has made it appear a good deal deeper than it actually is. The decoration of the barrel vault is also magnificent.

THE PAULINE CHAPEL

The Sala Regia gives access to the **Pauline Chapel,** built by **Antonio da Sangallo** for Paul III. Its lateral walls are decorated with frescoes by Michelangelo: the **Conversion of St. Paul** and the **Crucifixion of St. Peter.**

The Pauline Chapel - Interior.

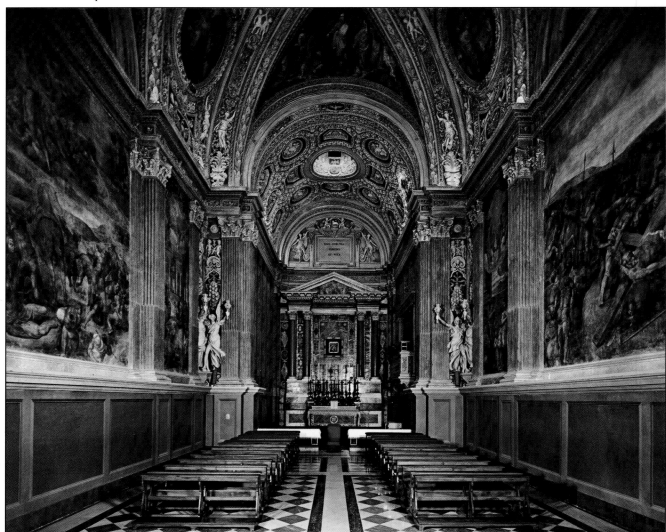

The Pauline Chapel - The Crucifixion of St. Peter (Michelangelo).

The Vatican Museums

The entrance to the Vatican Museums is on the Viale del Vaticano. From here the various sections of the Museums are reached by ascending the impressive double-helicoidal staircase: to our left are the Museums of Antiquities, straight ahead the Pinacoteca or Picture Gallery, and to our right the Museo Gregoriano Profano and Museo Pio-Cristiano.

MUSEUMS OF ANTIQUITIES

Comprehensively they represent the richest collection of classical art in the world. The collection is owing to the interest taken by various Popes, such as Clement XIV, Pius VI, Pius VII and Gregory XVI who reorganized and extended the collection of antiquities already amassed during the Renaissance.
Starting out from the Vestibolo dei Quattro Cancelli, we come to the large courtyard know as the **Cortile della Pigna.** This derives its name from the colossal bronze pine-cone placed on the double-stairway under the semicircular niche at one end of the courtyard. It comes from the Baths of Agrippa, and was used as an ornament of an ancient fountain. The pine-cone, which is mentioned in Dante's *Inferno*, is flanked by two bronze peacocks.

GREGORIAN EGYPTIAN MUSEUM

Founded by Pope Gregory XVI in 1839, it contains interesting remains, wooden mummy-cases, some of them painted, mummies and various artefacts relating to the art and civilization of ancient Egypt. The most fascinating collections on display are the carved scarabs, an essential component of the life of ancient Egypt, and mementos of its most important events, and the fine series of wooden mummy-cases. The Museum's holdings also include some impressive Egyptian statues, including the **statue of queen Tuia** (mother of Rhamses II), that of **Naophoros Psammeteksemb,** portraying a priest holding a temple in his hands, and the numerous statues representing the **goddess Sekmet.**
Worth noting, among the collection of papyri, is the famous **Vatican Book of the Dead,** a precious papyrus containing inscriptions relating to the cult of the dead.
In Room IV is a **wooden coffer of queen Hetep-heretes.** Room X (or Sala Grassi) houses the collection which Pope Pius XII received as a gift from the Grassi family.

PIO-CLEMENTINE MUSEUM

The collection derives its origin from the interest taken by Popes Clement XIV and Pius VI, from whom it derives its name. Both enriched and augmented the already-existing collection of ancient sculptures situated in the Cortile del Belvedere. Our description of the Museum will start out from the Vestibolo Quadrato (Room XII) and proceed in reverse so as to follow the itinerary prescribed inside the Museum.

Gregorian Egyptian Museum - 1st room.

VESTIBOLO QUADRATO - It contains the sarcophagus of a grandfather of Scipio Africanus: **L. Cornelius Scipio Barbatus.**

CABINET OF APOXYOMENOS - It is named after the statue of the athlete in the act of wiping away the sweat (*apoxyomenos*) with a strigil, the curved blade use in Greek and Roman antiquity to clean the skin after exercise. The statue is a Roman copy of the 1st century A.D. from the original by Lysippos.

This is followed by **Bramante's Spiral Stairway** built at the beginning of the 16th century.

We now enter the octagonal **Cortile del Belvedere**. This courtyard with a fountain at its centre, originally square in plan, housed the first sculptures placed here by Pope Julius II and was subsequently embellished with further ancient works of art of primary importance. The octagonal Ionic portico surrounding the courtyard opens out into four aediculae or cabinets containing sculptures and statues of notable artistic interest.

CABINET OF LAOCOON - This wonderful marble group, sculpted by Hagesandros of Rhodes and his sons Athanadoros and Polydoros, was discovered close to the Domus Aurea on the Esquiline in 1506. The statue, considered a masterpiece of Hellenistic art, represents the priest **Laocoon and his sons** enveloped by two snakes. A well-known episode of the *Aeneid* tells how Laocoon warned the Trojans about the threat posed by the wooden horse of the Greeks and how the goddess Athena, in anger, sent the snakes as a punishment against him. Recently the statue of the Laocoon has been restored by the insersion of a new arm, using the original fragment discovered by the archaeologist Pollak at the beginning of the present century.

CABINET OF APOLLO - The famous statue of the **Apollo Belvedere** is a Roman copy of the Greek original dating to the 4th century B.C. Found at Grottaferrata in the late 15th century, it portrays the youthful and beautiful son of Zeus, and symbolizes the divinity of human form and the self-perfection and triumph of man.

CABINET OF PERSEUS - The cabinet takes its name from the beautiful **statue of Perseus Triumphant**, an early 19th century sculpture by Antonio Canova. It represents Perseus with the head of Medusa, queen of the Gorgons, in his left hand. Statues of the two pugilists **Kreugas** and **Damoxenos,** also sculpted by Canova, stand beside it.

CABINET OF HERMES - It contains the beautiful **statue of Hermes,** a copy of the original bronze by Praxiteles.

ROOM OF THE ANIMALS - The sculptures displayed in this large rectangular room, mainly of animals, were in large part either sculpted or restored by Francesco Antonio Franzoni in the 18th century. Worth noting are: the **statue of Meleager** with dog and head of a slain boar,

The Belvedere Courtyard.

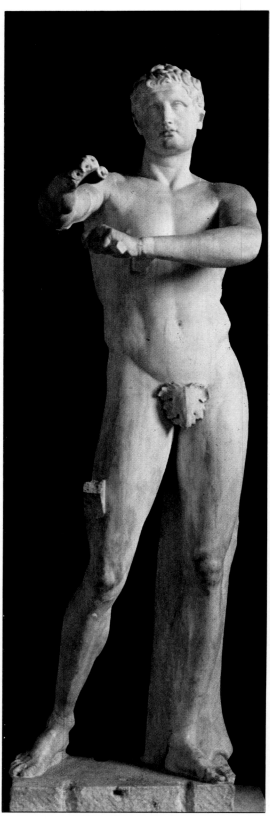

The Belvedere Courtyard.
The Apollo Belvedere.

Pio Clementine Museum.
Statue of Apoxyomenos.

The Belvedere Courtyard - The Laocoon Group.

The Belvedere Courtyard - The Torso Belvedere.

a copy of the 4th century B.C. original; the **Triton with Nereids and Cupids**; and the group of **Mithras killing the bull**. According to myth, the blood, the marrow and the semen of the animal fructified the earth and ensured plants and animals of fertility. Also on display in the room are some fine mosaics and a **crab** carved out of green jasper.

GALLERY OF THE STATUES - The gallery was laid out in its present form by the architect A. Dori for Pope Clement XIV, adapting and transforming the ancient loggia of the summer-house of Innocent VIII, and using it to house an interesting collection of ancient statues and busts. The most famous sculptures on display include: the **statue of Ariadne sleeping**, a replica of the 2nd century B.C. original; the **Apollo Sauroctonos** (Apollo watching a lizard), a copy of the bronze original by Praxiteles; and the **Barberini Candelabra**. These latter were found in Hadrian's Villa (at Tivoli) and rest on beautiful pedestals decorated with bas-reliefs. Other statues worth noting in the Gallery are: the statue of **Hermes**; that of the **injured Amazon**; the **portrait of Menander**; and the so-called **Eros of Centocelle** or "Genius of the Vatican", a Roman copy of the 4th century B.C. original.

HALL OF BUSTS - Situated at the foot of the Gallery of the Masks, the hall is divided into three sections in which are housed a series of ancient busts of considerable artistic importance. They include the **portraits of Cato and Portia**; the **head of Caracalla**; the busts of various **emperors**, such as **Julius Caesar, Marcus Aurelius and Trajan**; and the seated **statue of Jupiter** from the Palazzo Verospi.

GALLERY OF THE MASKS - We now retrace our steps to the Gallery of the Masks, a name it derives from the four wonderful **mosaics** with masks from Hadrian's Villa which decorate its floor. A number of famous statues are displayed in this gallery, first and foremost the **Venus of Cnidos**, a copy of the original by Praxiteles. The statue represents Aphrodite, goddess of love, in all the beauty of her nakedness, laying her garment over a vase before descending into the water. The sculpture is surrounded by an indefinable aura of fascination that the goddess emanates from her movements and her celebrated beauty. Also worth noting are the **Group of the Three Graces** (2nd century A.D.) and **Venus at the bath**.

ROOM OF THE MUSES - The highlight of the antiquities on display in this room is undoubtedly the so-called **Torso Belvedere**. This mutilated headless statue, influential during the Renaissance, also aroused the interest and admiration of Michelangelo, who carefully studied its powerful representation of the musculature of the human body. It perhaps represents Hercules and is signed by Apollonios, son of Nestor of Athens. It dates to the 1st century B.C. Also on display are the **statues of the Muses**, the **statue of Apollo** and a number of busts representing famous thinkers and poets: **Homer, Plato, Sophocles, Epicurus, Socrates** and others.

SALA ROTONDA - This impressive circular room was built by the architect Michelangelo Simonetti in 1780. It is surmounted by a hemispherical cupola evidently inspired by the Pantheon.

Very striking is the beautiful Roman **mosaic from the Baths of Otricoli** which decorates its floor. At the centre of the room is an enormous porphyry basin from the Domus Aurea. The most interesting sculpture in the room is, however, the **Jupiter from Otricoli**, a bust of the father of the gods evidently copied from the Greek original by Bryaxis. Other colossal statues are arranged round the walls of the room; they include the **statue of Antinous** from Hadrian's Villa; that of the **emperor Claudius**; and a magnificent statue of an unspecified female deity.

ROOM OF THE GREEK CROSS - Again built by Simonetti, this room in the neoclassical style is in the shape of a Greek cross. Note the bust of Pius VI, founder of the museum. A number of precious mosaics and fine imperial statues (including **Gaius Caesar** and **Lucius Verus**) decorate the room. But the two most conspicuous works on display are two huge **porphyry sarcophagi**: the one of **Constantia**, daughter of Constantine, and the other of **St. Helena**, mother of Constantine. Both are sculpted from monolithic blocks of Egyptian porphyry, carved with various figures: the former is decorated with scenes of wine-harvesting *erotes,* peacocks and delicate ornamental motifs; the latter, with scenes of Roman horsemen galloping in triumph over barbarian prisoners on their knees.

Pio Clementine Museum - Room of the Greek Cross.

Below and right-hand page: Chiaramonti Museum - New Wing - The Nile.

Founded by the Chiaramonti Pope Pius VII and laid out by Antonio Canova, the Museum consists of three sections: the Museo Chiaramonti proper, the Braccio Nuovo (or New Wing) and the Galleria Lapidaria.

The **Museo Chiaramonti** itself is displayed in part of Bramante's long gallery linking Innocent VIII's Palazzetto and the Papal Palace. It contains a collection of ancient art of considerable artistic value and historical interest, comprising ancient reliefs, sarcophagi, busts, statues and herms. The walls of the gallery are divided into 30 bays on each side. Also worth noting are the charming lunettes above, painted in the neoclassical style in the early years of the 19th century. Among the most striking of the antiquities on display are: the **sarcophagus of C. Junius Euhodus** and **Metilia Acte;** the so-called **Herm of Hephaistos,** husband of Aphrodite with the typical felt cap worn by craftsmen in ancient Greece; the funerary **monument of P. Nonnius Zeto;** and a fragment representing **Penelope**, wife of Ulysses.

THE BRACCIO NUOVO

Built by Raphael Stern between 1817 and 1822, the Braccio Nuovo (or New Wing) consists of a long gallery, whose walls open out into a series of deep niches for the display of ancient statuary. The floor of the hall is decorated with ancient mosaics, and its ceiling is magnificently coffered.

Among the masterpieces of ancient sculpture on display in this gallery are the following: the **portrait of Julius Caesar,** flanked by two bronze peacocks which adorned the atrium of the old St. Peter's during the Middle Ages; the **Hellenistic statue of the Nile,** found close to the church of Santa Maria sopra Minerva in 1513, with cherubs clambering over the recumbent river-god and scenes of Nilotic life and fauna represented on the plinth below; the famous **Augustus of Prima Porta** from the Villa of Livia on the Via Flaminia; the beautiful female figure known as **Pudicitia** from the Villa Mattei; the **statue of Demosthenes,** a copy of the bronze original by Polyeuctos; the **statue of the wounded Amazon;** and the statue of an athlete known as the **Doryphoros,** a copy of the original bronze by Polycleitos.

THE GALLERIA LAPIDARIA

Occupying the long gallery that marks the continuation of the Museo Chiaramonti, its holdings represent the most precious epigraphic collection extant, comprising over 5000 inscriptions: Christian ones to the right, pagan ones to the left. A series of sarcophagi, cippi and funeral altars are also on display.

SALA DELLA BIGA

Situated on the upper floor directly over the Atrio dei Quattro Cancelli, this circular, domed room was built by Giulio Camporese for Pope Pius VI. It derives its name from the magnificent white marble chariot (*biga* in Italian), placed at its centre. Only the body of the chariot and part of the horse on the right are antique; the remainder was added by the 18th century sculptor Francesco Antonio Franzoni. The chariot was previously used as an episcopal throne in the church of San Marco. Also worth noting is the **statue of Dionysos,** a copy of a Greek original. The room also houses two statues of the **Discobolus** or discus-thrower, and a number of fine sarcophagi.

Vatican Museum - Sala della Biga.

Right-hand page: Vatican Museum - Sala della Biga - The Discobolus.

GREGORIAN ETRUSCAN MUSEUM

Founded by Pope Gregory XVI in 1837, it occupies nine rooms and comprises interesting archaeological material excavated from some of the great Etruscan cemeteries: sarcophagi, bronzes, cinerary urns, terracottas and precious collections of Etruscan goldsmith's work.

Room 1 (Sala dei Sarcofaghi): the sarcophagi on display include that of the massacre of the **Niobids** and that of the **Magistrate.**

Room 2 (Sala della Tomba Regolini-Galassi): it takes its name from the famous Regolini-Galassi Tomb found at Cerveteri in 1836, and datable to the mid-7th century B.C. This large tomb under a tumulus was intended for a high-ranking couple, who were buried with large quantities of rich and precious grave-goods, including a magnificient golden **fibula.**

Room 3 (Sala dei Bronzi): divided into three sections, this room contains funerary and other bronzes found during excavations of Etruscan sites in the early years of the 19th century. Also on display are candelabra, statuettes, vases and the famous bronze statue known as the **Mars of Todi** dating to the 5th century B.C., and found on 2 June 1835.

Room 4 (Sala delle Urne): it contains a valuable collections of terracottas and cinerary urns from Volterra, Chiusi and Perugia.

Room 5 (Sala Guglielmi): named after the marchese Benedetto Guglielmi who donated the collection to Pius XI, the room contains some notable Etruscan *bucchero* (black burnished ware), bronzes and Greek painted vases.

Room 6 (Sala dei Preziosi): it contains some magnificent specimens of Etruscan goldsmithery (diadems, necklaces, earrings, etc.). Also particularly striking is the magnificent **head of a horse** made from amber.

Room 7 (Sala delle Terrecotte): it houses a collection of great interest comprising votive objects, urns, vases, statuettes and terracottas donated by the faithful in thanksgiving for divine help received.

Room 8 (Antiquarium Romanum): divided into three small rooms, the collection on display consists of helmets, ivories, Roman glassware, small vases and the head of an emperor dating to the 3rd century.

Room 9 (Sala Falcioni): acquired by Leo XIII at the beginning of the century, this important collection comprises Etruscan and Roman bronze objects mainly found in the territory of Viterbo.

ROOMS OF THE GREEK ORIGINALS

The three small rooms that follow contain a distinguished collection of sculptures and marbles of the Greek classical period. The finest of the pieces on display include: the **Palestrita Stele,** a funerary stele of the 5th century B.C., carved with a relief of a young athlete with arm upraised and, before him, a servant who is handing him a vase of oil for anointing his body; the **head of Athena**, a fragment of an ancient statue from Magna Graecia; and three interesting **fragments** from the Parthenon in Athens.

We now visit the **Collection of Vases,** comprising fictile material mainly from Etruscan tombs in southern Etruria. The collection is displayed in five rooms (**Sala della Meridiana, Sala Astarita, Emiciclo, Emiciclo Superiore, Sala dei Vasi Italioti**).

THE GALLERY OF THE GEOGRAPHIC MAPS

Designed by the architect Ottaviano Mascherino, this long corridor was decorated, under Pope Gregory XII, with 32 painted geographical maps depicting the regions of Italy and its islands, in its ancient and modern configuration. This extraordinary cartographical monument was the work of the cosmographer Ignazio Danti who produced it in the space of three years (1580-83).

GALLERY OF THE TAPESTRIES

This Gallery (the **Galleria degli Arazzi**) was formerly hung with the ten precious tapestries based on cartoons by Raphael currently displayed in the Vatican Picture Gallery. It is now decorated with ten others in replacement of them. These are the series known as the "New School". Produced in Bruxelles by Pieter van Aelst, they represent scenes from the New Testament and are based on cartoons by pupils of Raphael.

Gregorian Etruscan Museum
Sala delle Terrecotte.

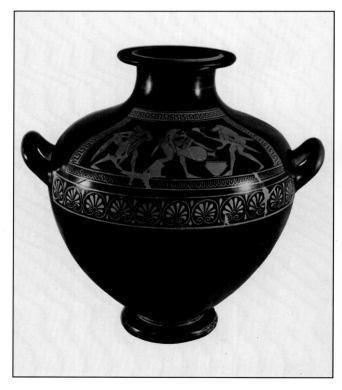

GALLERY OF THE CANDELABRA

To the right of the Sala della Biga is the beginning of the Gallery of the Candelabra. It takes its name from the candelabra placed in front of the arcades, at one time open, but closed under the pontificate of Pius VI. The Gallery is divided into six sections by arches.

Section I: the sculptures include a **sleeping Satyr;** the statuette of a **boy playing with walnuts;** and an interesting **sarcophagus of a boy.**

Section II: statue of Artemis Ephesina, an Anatolian deity, symbol of the fruitfulness of nature; a fine sarcophagus with reliefs of the myth of Protesilaos and Laodamia; and Roman **candelabra** datable to the 2nd century.

Section III: ancient candelabra (2nd century); and a **statue of Apollo** of archaic Greek type.

Section IV: sarcophagus with Bacchic scenes; and statue of a **boy with a goose,** a copy of the original by Boethos (3rd century B.C.).

Section V: contains a fine statue of a running girl, and an elaborately carved candelabrum from Otricoli.

Section VI: a statuette of Persephone; and a sarcophagus with a relief of the rape of the daughters of Leucippos (2nd century).

APARTMENT OF ST. PIUS V

The broad gallery decorated with ancient tapestries — the continuation of the Gallery of Geographic Maps — is only part of the Apartment of St. Pius V. Two other rooms form the Pope's apartment proper. Their walls are also hung with precious tapestries representing the Liberal Arts: "Dialectic", "Rhetoric" and "Grammar" (in the 1st Room); and "Arithmetic", "Music" and "Astronomy" (in the 2nd).

THE CHAPEL OF NICHOLAS V

We now visit the Chapel of Nicholas V (**Cappella Niccolina**). Built for the 15th century Pope Nicholas V, this small chapel is memorable for the magnificent frescoes by Fra Angelico that decorate its walls. The frescoes are divided into two series: **Scenes from the Life of St. Stephen** in the upper part, and **Scenes from the Life of St. Laurence** in the lower part. Dating to 1447-49, they are distinguished by the profound spirituality by which all the paintings of the Florentine Dominican artist are imbued.

Chapel of Nicholas V - Scenes from the life of St. Laurence (Fra Angelico).

The Maps Gallery

The Stanze of Raphael

The famous suite of rooms known as **Raphael's Stanze** was frescoed by the great artist of Urbino in 1508 (work began in the autumn of 1508). Pope Julius II was so impressed by the genius and imagination, and the sheer technical accomplishment with which **Raphael**, then only 25 years old, conceived this vast undertaking that he relieved the artists to whom he had previously entrusted the commission: Luca Signorelli, Pinturicchio, Sodoma and other distinguished painters of the time.

Let us now enter the first of the four rooms that comprise the Stanze:

ROOM OF THE FIRE IN THE BORGO - It is decorated with the famous fresco from which it takes its name, situated on the wall facing the window. The painting depicts the fire that swept through the Borgo — the district adjacent to the Vatican — in 847 and that was miraculously quenched by Leo IV by making the sign of the Cross. The fresco's effect derives in large part from the contrast between the two parts into which it is divided: in the foreground, people flee in terror from the flames, a young man carries his own father to safety and women bear vessels of water; in the background, the Pope stops the spread of the fire by making the sign of the Cross from the loggia of St. Peter's.

The other frescoes in the room are: the **Coronation of Charlemagne,** depicting the ceremony that took place in St. Peter's on 25 December 800; the **Battle of Ostia,** painted by Raphael's pupil Giulio Romano and illustrating Leo IV's victory over the Saracens; and the **Oath of Leo III,** it too painted by Giulio Romano.

The decorations of the ceiling of the room are by Perugino.

Raphael's Stanze - Room of the Fire in the Borgo:
The Fire in the Borgo.

STANZA DELLA SEGNATURA - This room was the private study and library of Pope Julius II and was the first in order of time to be frescoed. Its frescoes undoubtedly represent one of the most important and impressive works executed by Raphael in the course of his brief life. Their iconographic programme relates to the four principles of human knowledge: Theology, Philosophy, Poetry and Justice.

The first represents the **Debate on the Holy Sacrament,** better known under its Italian name the **Disputa.** The fresco is divided into two parts: below, the theologians and doctors of the Church discuss the nature of Truth; above, Christ, enthroned at the centre of a celestial hemicycle of the representatives of the Church triumphant, is flanked by his Mother and John the Baptist, with the Father above him. The link between the two spheres, the Church in its heavenly and earthly aspects, is represented by the host, the Holy Sacrament, on the altar.

On the opposite wall is Raphael's great treatment of philosophical knowledge: the **School of Athens.** At the centre of the fresco are Plato and Aristotle, the two greatest exponents of Greek thought. Among the other thinkers are Socrates among his followers, Heraclitus, below, and Diogenes lying on the steps.

In the lunette over the window is the fresco of **Parnassus,** corresponding to Poetry. The central figure is Apollo playing his lyre, surrounded by the Muses and the great poets of antiquity and modern times.

The fourth wall of the Stanza della Segnatura is dedicated to Justice: **Justinian receiving the Pandects** (Temporal Justice) and **Gregory IX approving the Decretals** (Spiritual Justice).

ROOM OF HELIODORUS - This room derives its name from the great fresco on the wall facing the entrance depicting **Heliodorus Cast out of the Temple.** Taken from an episode in the Book of Maccabees, the fresco represents Heliodorus who, having stolen the treasure from the Temple of Jerusalem, is assailed by a celestial horseman and two angels.

The other frescoes of the room, devoted to episodes in the history of the Papacy, represent: **Leo the Great stopping the Invasion of Attila;** the **Mass of Bolsena,** depicting the miraculous event that took place at Bolsena in 1263 when a Bohemian priest, hitherto sceptical about transubstantiation, found the consecrated host stained with blood, thus giving rise to the feast of Corpus Christi; and, in the lunette over the window, the **Liberation of St. Peter from Prison,** in which a radiant angel awakens the saint and leads him out of prison.

HALL OF CONSTANTINE - This room was completely frescoed by pupils of Raphael after the premature death of the master in 1520. The frescoes represent: **The Baptism of Constantine, the Battle of the Milvian Bridge,** the **Apparition of the Cross,** and the **Donation of Rome by Constantine to Sylvester I.**

Raphael's Stanze - The Stanza della Segnatura - Ceiling.

Raphael's Stanze - Stanza della Segnatura -
The School of Athens.

Raphael's Stanze - Stanza della Segnatura -
Debate on the Holy Sacrament.

Raphael's Stanze - Stanza della Segnatura: The Parnassus.

*Raphael's Stanze -
Room of Heliodorus:
Leo the Great stopping
the invasion of Attila.*

RAPHAEL'S LOGGE

After visiting Raphael's Stanze, we may enter the **Logge** or arcaded gallery designed by Bramante, completed by Raphael and frescoed by pupils of the artist (Giulio Romano, Giovanni da Udine, Gian Francesco Penni and others). The ceiling of the Logge is divided into thirteen bays, each containing four scenes taken from the Old and New Testament.

Left-hand page:
Hall of Constantine.

Raphael's Logge.

The Borgia Apartment

The residence of the Borgia Pope Alexander VI, the apartment consists of a suite of six rooms whose walls were frescoed by Pinturicchio and his pupils.

Room I (Sala delle Sibille) - The room, in which — tradition relates — Cesare Borgia murdered his brother-in-law (Lucrezia's husband), is decorated with 12 lunettes of **Sibyls** and **Prophets**.

Room II (Sala del Credo) - It derives its name from the 12 pairs of **Prophets** and **Apostles** bearing scrolls inscribed with verses of the ''Credo'' in the lunettes.

Room III (Sala delle Arti Liberali) - The room, with its magnificent 16th century fireplace, was frescoed with representations of the **Liberal Arts** by Antonio di Viterbo. The room was used by Alexander VI as his dining-room.

Room IV (Sala dei Santi) - Almost entirely decorated by Pinturicchio, the room is divided into a series of large lunettes containing beautiful frescoes, notable **St. Catherine before the Emperor Maximian**.

Room V (Sala dei Misteri) - Similar in form to the previous room, the lunettes that decorate the room were once again frescoed by Pinturicchio, this time with episodes from the life of Christ: the **Annunciation**, the **Nativity** the **Adoration of the Magi**, the **Resurrection** (with portrait of the kneeling Alexander VI), the **Ascension, Pentecost,** and the **Assumption of the Virgin**.

Room VI (Sala dei Pontefici) - The room takes its name from the names of various popes commemorated in the inscriptions in the lunettes. It is decorated with elaborate stuccoes and *grottesche* by Perin del Vaga and Giovanni da Udine, pupils of Raphael.

COLLECTION OF MODERN RELIGIOUS ART - Inaugurated by Pope Paul VI in 1973, it consists of over 600 works of painting and sculpture by leading artists of the 20th century. The 55 rooms housing the Collection in fact display works by such modern artists as **Modigliani, Le Corbusier, Chagall, Gauguin, Matisse, Manzù and Paul Klee.**

The Borgia Apartment - Ceiling.

The Sistine Chapel

Named after the Della Rovere Pope Sixtus IV for whom it was built, the Sistine Chapel is a large rectangular hall with a high barrel-vaulted ceiling. It was built by the architect Giovannino de' Dolci, based on a design by Baccio Pontelli, between 1475 and 1481. Both from an artistic and a religious and historical viewpoint, it represents one of the most important complexes extant. The Sistine Chapel is in fact the place where the most significant ceremonies in the life of the Church take place. The most famous of these is undoubtedly the election of the Pope through a meeting of Cardinals from all over the world which takes the name of the **Conclave.** This ceremony originated in the second half of the 13th century on the occasion of the election of the pontiff who was to become Pope Gregory X. At the time, the growing importance that the Papacy was coming to assume both politically and economically provoked bitter conflicts of interest between the various factions, each faction exerting the necessary pressure to ensure that its candidate were elected to the pontifical throne. This was compounded by the objective difficulty of assembling the College of Cardinals at short notice in Rome. The result of this state of affairs was that in 1268 the bishops who had gathered to elect the new Pope failed to reach a decision. Exasperated by this, and probably urged by St. Bonaventura, the citizens of Viterbo locked the bishops into the Papal Palace of the city in which the election was taking place that year, refusing them all contact with the outside world and thus obliging them to come to a speedy decision. Moreover, to preclude the possibility of any external influence, they obliged the bishops to communicate the eventual nomination by means of the by-now proverbial smoke-signal. Still today, in fact, thousands of faithful eagerly await the smoke signal that indicates the Conclave's result: if it is black, it means the Cardinals have failed to reach a decision and the Conclave continues; if it is white, it means that the nomination has been made.

No sooner had the construction of the Sistine Chapel been finished than Pope Sixtus IV obtained the services of the most illustrious painters of the period to decorate its ceiling and walls. They included **Pinturicchio, Perugino** and **Signorelli,** and the best-known exponents of the Florentine school such as **Botticelli, Ghirlandaio** and **Cosimo Rosselli**. As for Michelangelo's intervention, that dates to a period subsequent to the Chapel's initial decoration: in fact, the ceiling now covered by Michelangelo's wonderful scenes of the Creation, was originally frescoed by Matteo Serdenti with a simple pattern of stars set against an azure background, and with the coat of arms of the Della Rovere family placed at the ends of the vault.

Michelangelo's intervention has also obliterated the original iconographic scheme for the end-wall behind the altar, namely the two frescoes of the **Finding of Moses** and the **Nativity**, both by Perugino, which were later eliminated to make room for Michelangelo's monumental **Last Judgement.**

The choice of the subjects illustrated in the frescoes was not casual, since it was usual at that time to narrate the events of the Old and New Testament in pictorial terms to permit those of little education to gain a knowledge of the principal facts of religion without the aid of letters. Moreover, the individual frescoes have the peculiarity of accompanying the principal scene with one or more subsidiary episodes, though these are perfectly integrated with the main subject which is never lost sight of.

1st PAINTING: **The Circumcision of the Sons of Moses and Moses' Journey into Egypt.** The work is clearly of the Umbrian school. **Pinturicchio** and **Perugino,** who jointly painted the fresco, have here succeeded in conferring lightness and grace on the human figures, in spite of the painting's complexity. The delicate landscape in the background is attributable to the hand of Pinturicchio.

Ceiling of the Sistine Chapel - The Creation of Adam - Detail (Michelangelo).

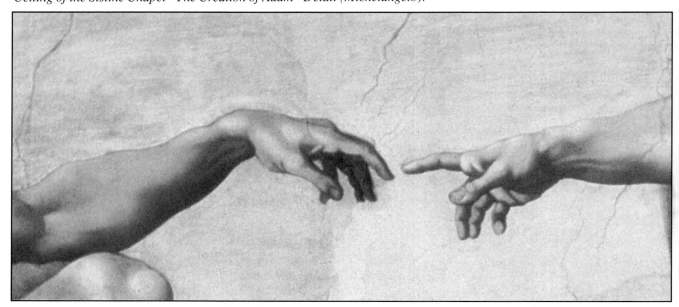

2nd PAINTING: **Moses in the Desert and the Burning Bush** and **Moses driving the Midianites from the Well, the Killing of the Egyptian and the Daughters of Jethro.** In this fresco by **Botticelli** particularly admirable are the female figures, especially the foreground group of the daughters of Jethro, and also the representation of the parable of the Burning Bush in the background, in which the calling of Moses is expressed both with force and reverence.

3rd PAINTING: **Crossing of the Red Sea** and **The Death of the Pharaoh with his Army (Cosimo Rosselli).** The choice of this subject was not determined merely by a wish to represent an episode from the life of Moses, albeit one of the most famous. It is almost certain in fact that this choice was also influenced by the wish to honour the religious crusade mounted by the reigning Pope. It was just before the decoration of the Sistine Chapel was begun that the Moslem Turks under Sultan Mohammed had attacked Rodi on the coast of Apulia and captured Otranto. Sixtus IV spared no energy nor expense in trying to expel the infidels from the peninsula, and succeeded in doing so the year following the attack (1481). That this contemporary event is alluded to in the fresco is proved by the inclusion of a portrait of Cardinal Bessarion, who is portrayed in the white-bearded man standing beside Moses with an urn in his hand. Bessarion had in fact warned the Pope and the faithful about the danger posed by the Moslem invasion and been the first to realize the need for a religious crusade.

4th PAINTING: **Moses receiving the Tables of the Law** and **The Worship of the Golden Calf.** This fresco, like the previous one, was painted by **Cosimo Rosselli**, undoubtedly a minor exponent of the Florentine school, but in some respects no less capable than his more illustrious colleagues.

5th PAINTING: **The Punishment of Korah, Dathan and Abiram (Botticelli).** This is a work that holds a distinctive place in the Tuscan master's oeuvre: it is all the more dark, dramatic and violent, in that the paintings of Botticelli we are used to admire are remarkable for their grace and charm, their aura of ecstatic mysticism. Yet Botticelli's treatment of the subject could hardly be bettered: the punishment meted out against those who had dared to elevate themselves above the Lord could not but be treated in a harsh and vehement way. To the left of the fresco, Dathan and Abiram are being swallowed up in the abyss opened in the earth beneath them, while Korah is falling to the ground together with his companions, doomed by the wrathful figure of Moses with his rod upraised at the centre. Behind him a faithful copy of the Arch of Constantine opens out on a beautiful landscape. The choice of the subject was also intended to stigmatize the attempt by the Dominican Archbishop Andrea Zamometic to call a Council at Basle with the purpose of undermining the position of supremacy of the Pope. Botticelli has included a self-portrait of himself among the crowd of onlookers to the right.

6th PAINTING: **The Reading of Moses' Testament** and **The Handing Over of the Rod, Symbol of Authority, to his Successor (Signorelli).** In the background of this fresco which concludes the series of paintings dedicated to the life of Moses, we see, to the right, the promised land and, to the left, the dying Moses. They are divided, at the centre, by Mount Nebo, on which an angel is indicating to Moses the site of Jerusalem and the "land of milk and honey" — a beautiful landscape of gentle hills and teeming waters — stretching behind them. Yet it is in the foreground that the two scenes that give their name to the painting are set: to the left, Moses hands over the rod of command to Joshua, while to the right a group of onlookers, lost in deep meditation, gathers round Moses to hear him read out his testament.

If the frescoes of the left wall are dedicated to the life of Moses, saviour of Israel, those of the right wall illustrate episodes from the life of Christ, saviour of mankind. Let us examine these, too, in turn:

1st PAINTING: **The Baptism of Christ.** The first fresco of the series, to the right of the altar, is attributed to **Pinturicchio** assisted by the other leading exponent of the Umbrian school of the day: **Perugino.** At the centre of the fresco is the scene of the Baptism of Jesus from which the painting takes its name. The gentle expressions of the onlookers, the soft colours with which the figures are painted, their meditative poses and attitudes of reverence and contemplativeness, imbue the painting with a deep sense of spirituality.

Sistine Chapel - Moses driving the Midianites from the Well, the Killing of the Egyptian and the Daughters of Jethro - Detail (Botticelli).

Sistine Chapel - Moses' Journey into Egypt (Pinturicchio and Perugino).

Sistine Chapel - Moses driving the Midianites from the Well, the Killing of the Egyptian and the Daughters of Jethro (Botticelli).

Sistine Chapel - Moses receiving the Tables of the Law and the Worship of the Golden Calf (C. Rosselli).

Sistine Chapel - The Punishment of Korah, Dathan and Abiram (Botticelli).

2nd PAINTING: **The Temptations of Christ** and **The Purification of the Leper (Botticelli).** In the foreground is the scene of purification, the one way of liberation from sin, to which Botticelli gives primary importance in the painting. Behind the altar is the façade of the hospital of Santo Spirito in Rome, built, like the Sistine Chapel, by Sixtus IV. The crowd of onlookers includes several portraits of contemporaries whom Botticelli was fond of introducing into his works. In the background to the right: Jesus drives off the devil from the summit of the mountain.

3rd PAINTING: **The Calling of the First Apostles (Domenico Ghirlandaio).** A painting imbued with a deep sense of reverence and love; in the background Christ is calling the first of the Apostles from the shores of Lake Galilee, while in the foreground St. Peter and St. Andrew kneel before Christ.

4th PAINTING: **The Sermon on the Mount** and **The Healing of the Leper (Cosimo Rosselli).** Though of lesser importance than the other paintings, it represents in a moving and effective way the concept of liberation from sin through forgiveness that so much characterizes the New Testament.

5th PAINTING: **Christ giving the Keys to St. Peter (Perugino).** The scene of Christ's delegation of authority to St. Peter, represented symbolically by the handing over of the Keys, is one of the most significant of the frescoes in terms of its subject-matter, and is remarkable for the masterly way in which Perugino has treated it. In the background we see (on the left) the payment of the tribute money and (on the right) the attempted stoning of Christ.

6th PAINTING: **The Last Supper (Cosimo Rosselli).** This is the last fresco of the cycle on the life of Jesus. In the background, like windows opening from the upper room, are scenes of the Agony in the Garden, the Capture of Christ and the Crucifixion.

It is clear from the succession of frescoes on both walls that the paintings are deliberately paired to point out the parallels and continuity between the Old and New Testament. Thus, the **Circumcision of the Sons of Moses** is paired with the **Baptism of Christ,** the **Reading of the Testament** with the **Last Supper,** and so on: the two sequences, the one representing the Old, the other the New Testament, are thus illustrated in parallel and an analogy drawn between the life of Moses and that of Christ.

Sistine Chapel - The Baptism of Christ (Pinturicchio and Perugino).

Sistine Chapel - The Temptation of Christ and ◄ the Purification of the Leper (Botticelli).

*Sistine Chapel - The Calling of the First Apostles
(D. Ghirlandaio).*

*Pages 68-69: Sistine Chapel
The Last Supper (C. Rosselli).*

THE LAST JUDGEMENT

Twenty-one years after the completion of the ceiling fresco, Michelangelo was once again called to work on the Sistine Chapel, this time to fresco the end-wall behind the altar with a representation of the **Last Judgement**. Begun in July 1536 and finished five years later, it constitutes one of the greatest masterpieces of the Renaissance. The scene describes with dramatic crescendo and great sense of movement, the expectation and turmoil of all the figures surrounding the dominating figure of Christ at the centre, severe and implacable in his role as Judge. Below, to the right, we see the figures of the damned huddled together in the boat guided by Charon who is leading them to the underworld. Above them, seated on clouds, the angels sound the trumpets of judgement. Seated below Christ's feet are Saints Laurence and Bartholomew, the latter with the emblems of his martyrdom, the knife and flayed skin, the face of which is a self-portrait of the artist himself. Particularly gentle and delicate, amid these scenes of wrath, is the figure of the Virgin at Christ's side.

Sistine Chapel - The Last Judgement - Detail of Christ the Judge and the Virgin Mary (Michelangelo).

Right-hand page:
Sistine Chapel - The Last Judgement (Michelangelo).

Sistine Chapel -The Last Judgement
Above: Detail of the left-hand lunette (Michelangelo).
Below: Detail of the right-hand lunette (Michelangelo).

Sistine Chapel - The Last Judgement -
Detail: St. Peter (Michelangelo).

THE SISTINE CHAPEL: THE CEILING

The painting of the ceiling of the Sistine Chapel was commissioned from Michelangelo by Pope Julius II. Michelangelo completed the frescoing of the vault between May 1508 and October 1512. This huge and complex work, though consisting of various scenes, is incredibly unified and homogeneous in its overall effect. Dividing the enormous surface area of the ceiling into a series of separate fields, Michelangelo placed the twelve colossal figures of **Prophets** and **Sibyls** right round its sides. He alternated the figures of the Prophets with those of Sibyls because they too, in the pagan world, had predicted the coming of a different era characterized by what was to be the Christian view of man and human life. The central part of the ceiling, its separate panels divided by the beautiful reclining nudes known as the **Ignudi**, represents a sequence of scenes from Genesis. In painting them, the artist did not follow the order in which they present themselves to the spectator on entering the Sistine Chapel. In fact, he painted them in reverse order, but in listing them below we follow the chronological sequence visible from the door by the altar:

—**The Creation of Light**
—**The Creation of Plants and of Stars**
—**The Separation of Land and Water**
—**The Creation of Adam**
—**The Creation of Eve**
—**The Fall and Expulsion from Paradise**
—**The Sacrifice of Noah**
—**The Flood**
—**The Drunkenness of Noah.**

The two pendentives to the side of the prophet Jonah are frescoed with scenes of **The Brazen Serpent** (to the right) and **The Punishment of Haman** (to the left), while the corresponding pendentives on the other side of the ceiling, separated by the Prophet Zachariah, illustrate **David and Goliath** and **Judith and Holofernes.** The spandrels and lunettes over the windows are frescoed with the Ancestors of Christ.

On this page: General view of the vault of the Sistine Chapel (Michelangelo).
Pag. 76-77: "The Creation of Adam".
Pag. 78-79: "The Creation of Eve".
Pag. 80-81: "The Fall and the Expulsion of Adam and Eve from the Garden of Eden".

Prophets and Sibyls on the vault of the Sistine Chapel (Michelangelo).
Above: The Prophet Daniel - The Sibyl of Cumae - The Prophet Isaiah.
Below: The Erythraean Sibyl - The Prophet Ezechiel - The Persian Sibyl.

The Vatican Library

Founded by Pope Sixtus IV in 1475, the Vatican collection has been progressively augmented and enriched in the course of the centuries. Between 1587 and 1589 the architect Domenico Fontana built a large hall to accommodate the library for Pope Sixtus V. Known as the **Salone Sistino** after the Pope who had commissioned it, this consists of a three-aisled hall delimited by seven pillars and decorated with frescoes depicting episodes from the pontificate of Sixtus V. A series of autographs of important personages of culture and history, illuminated manuscripts, books and codices, and other of the Library's priceless holdings, are on view in the display-cases of the Salone Sistino.

SALA DEGLI INDIRIZZI DI PIO IX: the name of this room derives from its original purpose, which was that of gathering together the testimonies of homage to the popes expressed by devotees throughout the world and of keeping a record of their addresses.

CHAPEL OF ST. PIUS V: this small private chapel was erected in the period 1566-1572, and decorated with frescoes depicting episodes from the life of St. Peter Martyr by Jacopo Zucchi.

SALA DELLE NOZZE ALDOBRANDINE: leading off from the Sala degli Indirizzi, this room is named after an ancient fresco depicting the nuptials of Alexander the Great and Roxana. The painting, known as the **Nozze Aldobrandine**, was found in the gardens of the Villa Aldobrandini on the Esquiline in 1605.

SALA DEI PAPIRI: its display-cases now containing ancient glassware, this room was designed to house a collection of ancient papyri.

MUSEO SACRO: founded by Benedict XIV in 1756, it contains a collection of Early Christian antiquities.

GALLERY OF URBAN VIII: a series of interesting scientific instruments are displayed here.

There follow the **SISTINE ROOMS (Sale Sistine)** designed to house archival documents, the **SALONE SISTINO** we have already described, and the **PAULINE ROOMS (Sale Paoline),** frescoed by Ricci in the 17th century.

The sequence of rooms continues as follows:

SALA ALESSANDRINA: created towards the end of the 17th century, it is named after the Pope in honour of whom it was built: Alexander VIII. The frescoes recount episodes from the life of Pius VI.

GALLERIA CLEMENTINA: named after the Pope who commissioned it, Clement XII, the Gallery was divided into five sections by Pius VI, and was frescoed by Domenico De Angelis with episodes from the life of Pius VII (1818).

The Vatican Apostolic Library.

The Vatican Picture Gallery

MUSEO PROFANO: begun under Clement XII, this small museum contains antiquities of various periods: Etruscan, Roman and medieval. Worth noting is the furniture designed by Valadier.

The Vatican Picture Gallery (**Pinacoteca Vaticana**) comprises a collection of paintings ranging in date from the 11th to the 18th century. The sixteen rooms in which the Gallery is displayed include masterpieces of painting by leading Italian and foreign masters. The modern building in which the Gallery is now housed was commissioned by Pope Pius XI, built by the architect Luca Beltrami and inaugurated in 1932. Some of its rooms are also occupied by a well-stocked library, offices and laboratories for restoration and conservation. But the main nucleus of the collection dates back a good deal earlier: it goes back to the time of Pius VI who in the second half of the 18th century gathered together the various paintings bequeathed by his predecessors in order to display them to the public. The Treaty of Tolentino (1797), however, deprived the collection of its most important pieces — they were shipped to France on Napoleon's orders — and it was only thanks to the efforts of Antonio Canova, the Inspector General of Fine Arts, that the works could be recovered and returned to the Vatican after the Congress of Vienna.

ROOM I: The Primitives - In this room are displayed the important collection of so-called "primitive" masters, comprising paintings in the byzantinizing style dating to the period antecedent to Giotto. Striking among the works on display is the **Last Judgement**, a painting of the Roman Benedictine school dating to the late 11th century; unusually circular in form, the panel's real artistic importance only emerged once it had been properly cleaned and its colours revealed in all their beauty. The **Portrait of St. Francis**, a work by Margaritone da Arezzo of the 13th century, is also noteworthy.

ROOM II: School of Giotto and Late Gothic Masters - The room is dominated by the **Stefaneschi Triptych**, attributed, at least in part, to Giotto but completed by his pupils.

ROOM III: Fra Angelico, Filippo Lippi and Benozzo Gozzoli - The personality of Fra Angelico, the 15th century Dominican whose purity and spirituality transpires from all his paintings, dominates the room. Here he is represented by the small but exquisite **Virgin between St. Domenic and St. Catherine** and **Episodes from the Life of St. Nicholas of Bari**. Angelico's pupil, Gozzoli, is in turn represented by the **"Madonna of the Girdle"**, with **Scenes from the Life of the Virgin** in its predella. The wonderful triptych of the **Coronation of the Virgin** is by Filippo Lippi.

The Square Garden and Art Gallery.

Vatican Picture Gallery - The Stefaneschi Triptych (Giotto).

ROOM IV: Melozzo da Forlì - The room, wholly dedicated to this distinguished 15th century artist, contains among other works **Sixtus IV and Bartolomeo Platina,** depicting the Pope's appointment of the historian Platina as Prefect of the Apostolic Library, and a fragment representing **Music-Making Angels.**

ROOM V: Various 15th Century Masters - The works on display include the **Pietà** by the German painter Lukas Cranach and, especially, the **Miracles of St. Vincent Ferrer** by Francesco del Cossa.

ROOM VI: Polyptychs - Carlo Crivelli is here represented by a **Madonna and Child** (1482), a wonderful work imbued with all the charm, elegance and softness of this Venetian artist. Antonio Vivarini's polyptych in a richly carved gothic frame may also be noted.

ROOM VII: Umbrian Paintings of the 15th Century - The room contains works of the Umbrian school, notably the **Madonna and Child Enthroned with Saints**, an altarpiece by Perugino, originally destined for the Palazzo del Comune in Perugia. Pinturicchio is also represented by two works: a **Madonna and Child** and a **Coronation of the Virgin.**

ROOM VIII: Raphael - This room undoubtedly represents the cornerstone of the collection, both in view of the artist's fame, and the representativeness of the three altarpieces displayed here, all dating to different periods in Raphael's life. The earliest of them is the **Coronation of the Virgin**, painted when the artist was only twenty years old and still under the influence of Perugino. It is followed by the **Madonna of Foligno** dating to 1511-12, and the sublime **Transfiguration,** painted by Raphael just before his premature death.

ROOM IX: Leonardo - The paintings on display in this room include an uncompleted work by the great Tuscan genius, the **St. Jerome,** and the **Pietà** by the Venetian master Giovanni Bellini, as well as interesting paintings by other Renaissance masters such as Lorenzo di Credi (Leonardo's contemporary).

ROOM X: Titian - The room is dominated by Titian's altarpiece of the **Madonna of San Niccolò dei Frari.** Painted for the church of the same name in Venice, the work is imbued with a deep sense of spirituality. Also of interest are two works by Paolo Veronese: the **St. Helen** and **Allegorical Scene.**

ROOM XI: Late 16th Century Masters - The most distinguished of the masters represented here is Federico

Barocci, three works by whom are on display: the **Madonna of the Cherries** (1573), the **Blessed Michelina** and **St. Francis receiving the Stigmata.**

ROOM XII: Caravaggio & the Bolognese School - Michelangelo Merisi better known as Caravaggio, one of the most brilliant and influential exponents of Italian painting in the 17th century, is here represented by his famous **Deposition** in which the intrinsic pathos of the subject is heightened by the dramatic lighting which materializes the figures in all their humanity and physicality. Also displayed in the room are famous works by Guercino (**Mary Magdalen**), Domenichino (**Communion of St. Jerome**) and Guido Reni (**Crucifixion of St. Peter**). There follow Rooms XIII and XIV, containing works of the 17th and 18th century, and Room XV, devoted to portraits. The latter include: **Portrait of Doge Niccolò Marcello** (Titian); **Portrait of Clement IX** (Carlo Maratta); and **Portrait of Benedict XIV** (Giuseppe Maria Crespi).

Having completed our tour of the Picture Gallery, we now begin our visit to the complex of museums formerly located in the Lateran Palace but recently transferred to the building parallel to the Pinacoteca Vaticana. The three Museums in question are:

THE MUSEO GREGORIANO PROFANO: Founded by Gregory XVI and moved to the Vatican by John XXIII, it contains Roman antiquities dating from the 1st to the 3rd century A.D., including urns, sarcophagi and Roman copies of original Greek statues of the 5th century.

THE MUSEO PIO-CRISTIANO: The Museum was instituted by Pope Pius IX and only installed in its present site in 1963. It comprises numerous Christian antiquities found in the Catacombs or preserved in churches.

THE ETHNOLOGICAL MISSIONARY MUSEUM: Inaugurated in 1927, it comprises artefacts relating to non-European cultures, donated by the Church's missions throughout the world or amassed on the occasion of the Missionary Exhibition in 1925. Transferred to the Vatican's Palazzo di San Callisto in 1963, the Museum was later (1969-70) moved to the building in which it is now housed.

THE HISTORICAL MUSEUM: Opened to the public in 1973, the Museum, founded by Pope Paul VI, is now housed in new rooms situated below the Giardino Quadrato. It contains magnificent carriages that once belonged to popes and prelates, and a fine collection of firearms. The historical relics on display also include memorabilia of the now-dissolved army corps of the Vatican State and uniforms and armour belonging to them.

Vatican Picture Gallery - Episodes from the life of St. Nicholas of Bari (Fra Angelico).

TEMPLA DOMVM EXPOSITIS·VICOS FORA MOENIA PONTES·
VIRGINEAM TRIVII QVOD REPARARIS AQVAM·
PRISCA LICET NAVTIS STATVAS DARE COMMODA PORTVS·
ET VATICANVM CINGERE SIXTE IVGVM·
PLVS TAMEN·VRBS DEBET·NAM QVAE SQVALORE LATEBAT·
CERNITVR IN CELEBRI BIBLIOTHECA LOCO·

*Vatican Picture Gallery - Sixtus IV and Bartolomeo
Platina (Melozzo da Forlì).*

*Right-hand page: Vatican Picture Gallery
- Music-Making Angel (Melozzo da Forlì).*

Left-hand page: Vatican Picture Gallery - The Transfiguration - Detail (Raphael).

Vatican Picture Gallery - The adoration of the Magi (Lo Spagna).

A section of the Vatican Gardens with the boat-shaped fountain.

Vatican Gardens - The Casina of Pius IV
- the great hall with vault decorations.

Vatican Gardens - The Casina of Pius IV
- the villa's open square with one of the entrance.

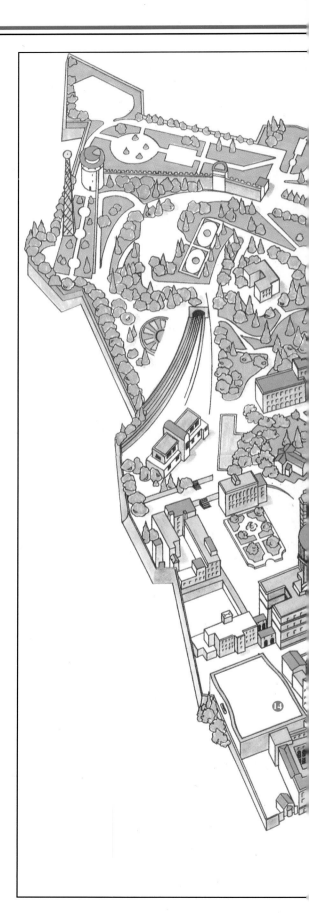